When Your Baby Dies Through Miscarriage or Stillbirth

Louis A. Gamino
and
Ann Taylor Cooney

Augsburg Books

WHEN YOUR BABY DIES THROUGH MISCARRIAGE
OR STILLBIRTH

Cover design by David Meyer; cover image from PhotoDisc, Inc.
Book design by Michelle L. N. Cook

Library of Congress Cataloging-in-Publication Data
Gamino, Louis A., 1953-
When your baby dies through miscarriage or stillbirth / Louis A. Gamino and Ann T. Cooney
p. cm.—(Hope and healing series)
ISBN 0-8066-4355-2 (alk. paper)
1. Perinatal death. 2. Miscarriage. 3. Stillbirth. 4. Bereavement—Psychological aspects.
I. Cooney, Ann T., 1947- II. Title. III. Series.
RG631.G36 2002
618.3'92—dc21 2001053548

The paper used in this publication meets the minimum requirements of American National Standard for Information Sciences—Permanence of Paper for Printed Library Materials, ANSI Z329.48-1984. ♾ ™

Manufactured in the U.S.A. AF 9-4355

06 05 04 03 1 2 3 4 5 6 7 8 9 10

Foreword

Grief, by definition, is painful—emotionally and spiritually. It is especially painful when associated with the loss of a baby through miscarriage, ectopic pregnancy, stillbirth, or newborn death. We may face more intense feelings and deeper doubts in these circumstances than we have ever experienced before.

This book by Louis Gamino, a clinical psychologist, and Ann Taylor Cooney, a clinical nurse specialist, reminds us that these turbulent feelings are to be expected—but that, with time and effort, we will adapt to our loss. Fully experiencing the wide range of emotions and eventually accepting what cannot be changed will gradually allow the storms of grief, anger, or uncertainty to subside.

Accepting what cannot be changed is possible when God is the foundation of our lives. But even that firm foundation can be shaken by the death of a baby. Questions about God are common during grief. **If you are struggling with your faith during this time, please talk with your pastor so that your doubts can be explored without guilt, and your faith can be restored and strengthened.**

One of the greatest predictors of effectively moving through grief is having a nurturing, supportive social network. Such a network of family members or friends provides the right blend of comfort and challenge at the appropriate times. For many people, this supportive social network is their Christian community where they have a common faith and hope, rooted in a loving and merciful God. Gathered around God's Word and Sacraments, Christians find strength to share one another's burdens and sorrows.

Holy Scripture records God's faithfulness to His children through many kinds of tragedies and losses. May you parents who have lost a baby be blessed with the gift of endurance to withstand the pain you feel. May you be further blessed with courage and strength to openly face your doubts and fears. May you be blessed with supportive friends to serve as human reminders of God's faithfulness to you in your grief. And, finally, may you find your faith renewed and receive the comfort that only God can bring through Christ.

– Rev. Leroy B. Joesten, Lutheran pastor and chaplain
Vice President, Mission and Spiritual Care
Advocate Lutheran General Hospital
Park Ridge, Illinois

Contents

Prayers of Comfort

If you have suffered the loss of a child through miscarriage, ectopic pregnancy, stillbirth, or newborn death, you may still be carrying deep wounds that no one else can fully understand. But God knows and understands. God is with you now though you may have doubts. God has not abandoned you, and never will. You can talk to God about your deepest woes and your angriest thoughts, and you will know that God is listening and offers you His love in Christ.

The foreword and the following prayers have been added to this book by Thrivent Financial for Lutherans to help you find words for your feelings and to bring you comfort. God, who gave His Son for your eternal well-being, will help you now. Go to God in faith and hope.

(Note: The prayers that follow were written by Jeannie Hannemann, founder of Elizabeth Ministry, an international movement designed to support women and their families throughout the joys, trials, and sorrows of the childbearing years (www.elizabethministry.com). The prayers have been edited by a Lutheran pastor especially for members of Thrivent Financial for Lutherans.)

Comfort Us, Lord

Dear Lord,

Never before have I felt this much pain. I feel overwhelmed and devastated.

This loss is more than the end of a pregnancy, more than a change in our plans—it is the death of our child. This profound sadness seems to bring up all previous losses.

People expect us to "get on with our lives." In so many ways, ours is an invisible tragedy. Only You, Creator God, know the deepest pain in our hearts and know the reality of our child.

Help us hold steadfast through the tears. Help us find meaning in living while facing the death of our baby. I feel disconnected from life in so many ways. Remember me, Lord, and keep me connected with You through Your Son, Jesus.

Guide me, God, out of the isolation I feel. Keep me from thoughts of blame. Open me up to the grief I must experience, and give me the strength to endure.

Give me courage to face the pain I see in the eyes of my spouse that is a reflection of my own. Embrace me with Your eternal love so that I may embrace my partner. Meld our broken hearts together in a love that can endure this tragedy—a love made complete in Your love for us through our Savior.

Comfort us, Lord, and show us the way to rest in Your love. Console us each as individuals and as a couple. Help us grow closer to one another and to You.

In Jesus' name I pray.

Amen.

A Mother's Prayer

Compassionate Lord,

I feel so empty now. I remember the excited feeling of new life growing within me. My baby and I were one. Now I am alone. That intimate togetherness is gone. The separation from my child is devastating. My womb aches with an intensity that brings me to my knees.

I am overwhelmed with my loss. I know people around me just don't understand. I want to be comforted, yet I feel myself push others away. Sometimes I think I'm going crazy. Nothing seems to make sense. Nothing seems important now. Lord, don't let me push You away, too. Rather, let me draw closer to You in Christ.

My husband seems to be withdrawing. He has thrown himself into his job and acts as if life is normal. Life will never be the same again. Will I ever have energy and direction again? All I can do is cry, sigh, and relive every detail of the pregnancy and miscarriage. I worry about our marriage. Provide us with the strength and commitment to reach out to one another and grow in our love. Strengthen our faith in You, so that in faith we can be strong for each other.

I see a pregnant woman and feel such jealousy. I read the birth announcements in the paper and my stomach churns. Even the television commercials for baby food bring a new flood of tears. Help me, Lord, to move out of the depths of despair. Guide me to a new perspective that does not forget my loss, but integrates it into healthy living. Teach me to move forward on the solid rock of Your love in Christ. Dry my tears in time, O God. Help me remember that in the eternal future in heaven, I will understand and there will be no tears.

Give me hope in Your resurrection. Though my baby has died to me, I commend my child to Your boundless love, for our risen Savior's sake.

Comfort me, Lord. I need Your peace.

Amen.

A Father's Prayer

I come before You with a heavy heart. I've held back my tears, attempting to be strong for my wife. It is difficult enough to face the death of my child, but watching my wife grieve is more than I can handle. I feel so helpless. How can I comfort her when my own heart is breaking?

Help me, Father, to help my wife. Give me the openness to offer her the tenderness of my tears. Help me to communicate my deepest feelings to her. I've heard these tragedies can either destroy a marriage or bring a couple closer together. Give us the wisdom to cling to each other and to You, and to draw strength from our love and Yours.

I even find myself jealous of my wife. She at least held our child in her womb. My arms are empty and so is my heart. Then there is the concern for my wife. People seem to think it is only the mother who grieves. Everyone always asks me the same question: "How is your wife doing?" No one asks how I'm doing! Don't they know it is also my baby who died? Don't they know I am also grieving? Just as You always forgive me, Lord, help me to forgive those who do not include me in their expressions of concern.

Lord, I would have been such a good father. All of my dreams and hopes associated with my child are shattered. I watched the news tonight and heard of a small child beaten by her dad. I screamed at You for allowing that man to have a child and mine is gone. It's not fair! My anger and grief seem unbearable. I want to blame someone, yet I know that is irrational. I feel there must be a way I can stop this horrible thing from happening to us. Nothing frustrates a man more than knowing he can't "fix" things.

O God, fill the void in my life with Your grace and goodness in Christ. Turn my thoughts heavenward. Settle my soul and help me find strength.

Amen.

Other Children in the Family

Loving Lord Jesus,

We know our other children need our attention. Give us the patience, strength and wisdom needed to parent them at this time. Help us to be sensitive to their pain and suffering.

The loss of a baby is a painful lesson in the miracle and fragility of life. Help us to convey that message in an age-appropriate manner.

Guide us in giving explanations that are simple. Keep us open to their questions and their needs. Help us lead them into Your loving arms for comfort.

I realize that children often believe their actions, thoughts or wishes are powerful enough to cause things to happen. Help me be attuned to any personal responsibility my children may feel toward the death of the baby. Before the death, they may have felt jealous that the new baby would get all the attention. Now, they may feel horribly guilty and responsible for the baby's death. Help me give assurances that nobody is to blame and that You have forgiven them for any bad thoughts they may have had.

This loss gives me a deeper appreciation for my other children. I thank You for them. I cherish each day with them. I know there are no guarantees tomorrow. Keep me from becoming overprotective and fearful for their health and safety. Send Your holy angels to watch over them.

Help us to include our children in the healing process so that they do not feel confused, left out, or not important enough to be included. Pull together all members of our family at this time of mourning. Bring us ever closer to You.

Amen.

About Grieving Grandparents

Help us, Lord.

It is so difficult to see my parents' grief. They were so excited about a new grandchild. Now they are at a loss for words. I know that they had expectations for their grandchild. They made plans for their relationship, just as we did. Somehow I feel I let them down. It was like giving them a gift and then taking it away.

I sometimes wish I could be a little child again and climb into the lap of my mother or father and be comforted. When I was little and hurt my knee, my mother would kiss it and make it all better. No kisses can make this better. For this, I need the touch of Your love and compassion.

I know my parents are hurting twice. They are hurting for their loss of a grandchild and hurting to see me in so much pain. It is so hard for them to watch us hurt.

I know I should be more comforting to them in their grief, but I just don't have the strength. So I'm asking You, Lord, to heal their broken hearts. Give them the courage to face this tragedy with You at their side and in their hearts.

Let me learn from their wisdom. It is a wisdom that was gained from their sorrows over the years. And may we all be made still wiser through the word and the work of Christ our Savior.

Help all of us transform our grief into compassion for each other. Comfort us by the compassion You have for us in Your Son Jesus.

Amen.

Painful Cliches

Dear Lord,

We know people mean to be helpful and comforting, but so often their words are negative and painful.

"It's for the better." No, it's not! This is not the way it is supposed to be. Parents are not supposed to outlive their own children. Still, I know Lord, that You will work this out for our good because You have promised.

"It's nature's way of getting rid of a mistake. There was probably something wrong, so be grateful it didn't live." Our baby wasn't a mistake! We unconditionally loved our child. We trust now in Your wisdom and love, O God.

"It's the will of God." We cannot believe that a loving God of compassion could ever will the death of a baby. In Genesis we hear of Your plan, Lord, for no sickness, pain or death. It was after Your creation that these troubles came into human lives. We believe that You grieve with us, and we look to You to ease our grief.

"God only gives us what we can handle." Is that supposed to mean that if I weren't such a strong person, my baby would still be alive? I know that isn't true. What my faith does tell me is that You, God, for Christ's sake, will give us the strength and support we need to handle whatever situation we face.

"There are more babies where that one came from; you can always have another." One child does not replace another. We pray for the blessing of other children, but know there are no guarantees that we will conceive again.

Help us, merciful God, move beyond people's words and feel their intent to comfort us. Let us understand that they simply do not know the right words to say. Let us be open to the embrace of their hearts so we may accept the blessings of their comfort. Finally, let the comfort of Your words and the grace of the Lord Jesus sustain us.

Amen.

Introduction

I am a father who has lost a child.

I recall vividly the pain I felt at the death of my newborn son, Anthony, and in the days thereafter. It was a deep, aching, helpless, wrenching pain. Tears welled up and broke through frequently. My voice cracked with emotion when I tried to speak. Friends' hugs were comforting but often led to even more tears. The sadness and grief were profound.

The fact that I knew in advance that my son would be born with fatal physical impairments did not lessen my grief. Being a clinical psychologist with special training in bereavement did not insulate me from the pain. My faith in God did not keep me from hurting. Loss of a child hurts—terribly and deeply.

Grief is a journey that you need not travel alone. This book is meant to be a gentle, comforting conversation along the way with someone who's been there. Talking with someone who understands your experience is a time-tested way of relieving pressure and pain. Someone who can help you put into words the rush of thoughts and feelings bombarding you right now.

So, when you're ready, read and listen. The first chapter is on miscarriage. The next chapter is on stillbirth and newborn death. Start with the chapter that applies best to your situation and read at your own pace.

This book is also intended for your family members. In chapter 5, my co-author, Ann Cooney, writes about her own experience of losing a sister through stillbirth. There is a section on grandparent grief as well.

We genuinely hope these pages will touch you in a way that eases your aloneness, helps you to recognize your emotions, and offers some perspective and guidance on the experience of losing a child.

—L.A.G.

Chapter 1

Miscarriage

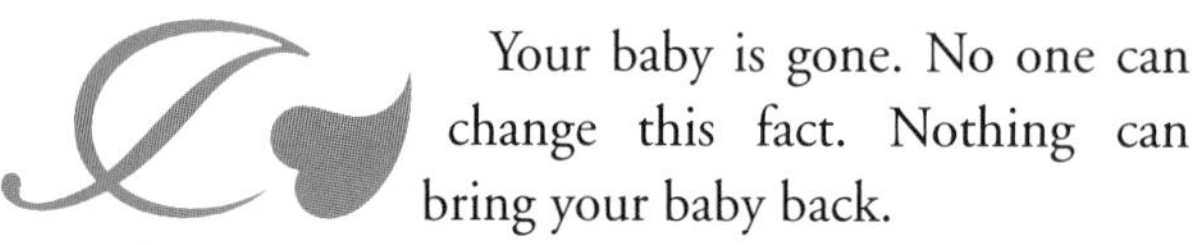

Your baby is gone. No one can change this fact. Nothing can bring your baby back.

This is the heartbreak of miscarriage. You were looking forward to being this child's parent. You were storing up love, ready to lavish it on this new child. You were ready to welcome her into your life and to cherish her with the love only a parent can give. Suddenly, before you even had a chance to really hold your baby, she slipped beyond your grasp. Now, all your expectations and hopes for this child are gone, and all your preparations seem pointless.

This is a critical time for you. There are phone calls to make. There are family and friends to contact. There are medical needs to address. You have to adjust to the changes—large and small. You may feel overwhelmed at the details. Everything is happening too quickly.

One mother described her feelings after her miscarriage by recalling an incident that happened when she and her husband were newlyweds. While swimming in a river, her wedding ring slipped off into the swift current. Despite their frantic searching, her ring was gone forever. She felt sickened, disappointed, and inconsolable. She valued her wedding ring tremendously. She blamed her own carelessness. Her husband tried to comfort her by offering to replace it. He meant well, but she became angry. It was her ring, and it was gone. To her, there was no replacement for the ring that symbolized their love and commitment. The loss of this intimate part of her life was the closest she could come to describing her anguish after her miscarriage.

When you became pregnant, you were entrusted with the precious life of a child to carry and care for. But the miscarriage means that this life ended just as it was beginning. At first, the loss is more than a person can comprehend and absorb. Questions outnumber answers. How could this happen?

The cascading emotions you feel are natural reactions: shock and disbelief, sadness, anger, protest, guilt, fear. You may feel all of these emotions or only some of them. You may experience several at once, or they may wash over you one at a time. Grief has no hard-and-fast rules, follows no timetables, and knows no calendars.

Slow down and take a few quiet moments to consider what is happening to you and how you can handle the events and emotions flooding you right now. Then, after this quiet time, you can make decisions and take the appropriate actions.

Did I Do Something to Cause This?

Miscarriage is a biological event that medical science has been unable to completely explain. Mothers often blame themselves. Perhaps these ideas spring from a desire for some control over what is largely uncontrollable. Most probably, your miscarriage was due to internal physical conditions that prevented the complete natural development of your baby. It probably was not a result of something you did or failed to do.

When a pregnancy is joyful and a child is much anticipated, miscarriage hits very hard. You wanted to hold on to this child, but he is gone. Even as your heart is breaking, you may feel that you will break into pieces, too.

On the other hand, a mother may be surprised at first by the pregnancy. She needs some time to get used to the idea of a new baby or how to make room in her life for another child. If so, a miscarriage may generate guilt because of the mother's initial mixed feelings. This may be true especially if voluntary termination of the pregnancy was ever considered. Some mothers conclude that the miscarriage could be a punishment for their unwelcoming or fearful attitude. Again, such feelings are irrational and represent a desire for control or understanding.

Was My Baby a Real Person When I Had the Miscarriage?

Miscarriage has a confusing and distressing aspect: There may be no recognizable "baby" in the mass of blood and tissue expelled from your body. You may be alone when the miscarriage happens. The life form is lost among the bloody material that is discarded. If your miscarriage occurred in a medical setting, sensitive health professionals can help you examine tissues for recognizable remains of your baby. When possible, view the physical remains. While at first this may seem morbid, this viewing gives you a better grasp of your baby's physical appearance and degree of development, and it later aids the grieving process.

If you were not able to view your miscarried baby, educational resources can help you visualize the wonder and fragility of the human embryo. Among the resources are science museum exhibits that show week-by-week fetal development, videos such as "The Miracle of Life" produced by PBS' NOVA series, or the magazine *As Your Baby Grows,* published by American Baby. These displays and materials help you get a better appreciation of how far your baby had grown, what she looked like, or how much she weighed. Then you can better understand what you have lost.

Many parents find comfort in the words of the Old Testament: "Before I formed you in the womb I knew you" (Jer. 1:5). Parents say this reminds them of God's providential plan for every person. Your miscarried baby was a precious creation despite her brief life.

Consider naming your child as a way of confirming her existence and value. Giving your baby a name is a fundamental way of conferring basic human dignity. Because the gender of your miscarried child may not be known, you may choose a name suitable for either a boy or girl. Should you decide to name your baby, include her name along with other family members in a family Bible or in genealogical records so that the entire family can help secure her place in your lives.

How Can I Remember Someone I Never Knew?

Among the biggest problems for parents following a miscarriage is the absence of memories. Because you never had the chance to hold your child in your arms or interact with her, you have no pleasant memories to fall back on as a source of comfort. When someone that we have known and loved for many years dies, we console ourselves with thoughts of the times we had together. After miscarriage, there is no chance for such memories to comfort you.

You do not have memories; you have lost possibilities. Not only has your child died, but your dreams for the future have died with him. Standing empty-handed while looking into a vision of possibilities may stir feelings of anger and protest. "Why me?" is a frequent lament. When my wife and I lost Anthony, due to his medical problems, I recall thinking: "Why us? We'd be good parents," and "Others are having healthy babies; why didn't we?" Such thoughts and feelings may be especially strong if you had trouble conceiving or were treated for infertility.

Why Don't Others Understand My Pain?

Others' reactions to your miscarriage may disappoint or even anger you.

Some would-be sympathizers may discount or minimize your loss by saying, "You can have another one." Having another child does not replace this miscarried baby, nor does it erase the confusion and pain of this loss. While it is easy to be angry at such comments, a simple reply is best: "We don't feel that way about it," or "This pregnancy was important to us; that's why we're grieving."

Consider the example of a family with four daughters. A miscarriage occurred between births of their living children. The mother related how others seem to overlook the fact of the miscarried pregnancy in light of her family's size. Looking at her four daughters playing together, the mother remarked wistfully, "I see the gap," referring to the fifth child that should have been there. Years later, she still wondered about what might have been had that child lived.

Parents who miscarry face the dilemma of whether to tell others and what to say. Maybe no one knew that you were pregnant. If others already knew, you may feel embarrassment or shame. Perhaps you did not have your family's wholehearted approval of the pregnancy or its timing. While there is no single solution to any of these dilemmas, the following considerations can help you approach various circumstances:

- People cannot be helpful to you if they do not know what your difficulty is. Confiding your feelings to a sympathetic relative or friend is usually soothing and healing.

- If you feel some people will not understand your pain, remember that you have no obligation to tell them. The choice is yours. For those who may not understand readily, saying something general is probably enough: "We were expecting a baby but lost her during pregnancy."

- The baby's father is hurting, too, even though the pain may reveal itself in different ways. At times like these, it is critical for both partners to be present for and tolerant of one another. Mutual love and respect permits each of you to grieve and brings you closer together at this time of crisis. Remember that you need each other, maybe more than ever. Chapters 3 and 4 go into more detail about this relationship.

How Do I Hold on to Memories of My Lost Child?

Creating a memorial to your lost baby is appropriate, even while your feelings may still be very raw. Parents find many creative ways to memorialize children. The important thing is that a memorial or keepsake helps preserve your child's memory and may help you feel closer to the child that was.

With miscarriage, parents often use symbols to remember a lost child. Some plant special trees or shrubs as a symbol of their baby's life or as an expression of their love. Sometimes a toy intended for the child becomes a special keepsake. Some place a marker in a cemetery even though the family has no remains to bury.

The healing power of the written word is helpful. Some parents write letters to their baby, compose poetry, or merely record their thoughts and feelings in journals. These writings can be a tremendous source of comfort later.

Points to Remember

1. The miscarriage was not the result of something you did or did not do, even if the pregnancy was a surprise to you at first.

2. When possible, view the remains. This helps your grieving process. If that is not possible, view pictures or videos of a developing fetus to help you understand your baby's development.

3. Naming the baby gives him or her human dignity. You may add this name to family registers and other genealogical information.

4. Disregard thoughtless comments from people who say, "You can have another baby." You don't have to explain yourself or talk about your miscarriage if you don't want to.

5. Confiding your feelings to a trusted friend or family member is an important step toward healing.

6. Remember the baby's father is grieving, too. This crisis time can bring parents closer together.

7. Plant a tree or hold dear a toy or keepsake as a way to remember your lost child.

8. Write letters to your baby, create a piece of poetry, or record your thoughts and feelings in a journal. These words will be of tremendous comfort later.

Chapter 2

Stillbirth and Newborn Death

You are reading this because you have lost a child due to stillbirth or newborn death, or know someone who has. Because these losses involve different circumstances, there is a brief section on each one. Some examples may be similar to your situation. In other ways, your loss is unique.

With all the advances in modern medicine, unanticipated stillbirth is a relatively rare event. More often, when stillbirth happens, your baby's death was detected before your delivery. Perhaps you were aware that your baby was not moving. Or, during a medical examination, your baby did not register a heartbeat. Diagnostic tests, such as ultrasounds, are used to confirm that your baby is not alive. Doctors may prefer for labor to begin spontaneously rather than inducing labor.

Thus, a mother finds herself in the sad situation of waiting to deliver a child she realizes has already died. Delivering a stillborn child is a labor of sorrow. Hearing the first cries of other infants being born in the hospital at the same time can be especially emotional.

When your child is stillborn, you have little warning and no chance to get ready or brace yourself. You feel blindsided, shocked, and caught totally off guard.

Everyone likes to believe the world is orderly, predictable, fair, and just. Sadly, this is not always so. Nothing seems quite so unfair as the death of an innocent child, especially one who is much loved and anticipated. Very often, intense feelings of frustration and rage well up inside when you realize that events are not meeting your hopes and expectations. Your sadness and grief may be clouded over by anger.

Why Do I Feel So Helpless After My Newborn Died?

First, read two very different stories of newborn death, both of which happened.

For the first couple, pregnancy was happily normal and free of complications. The mother experienced very few symptoms or discomforts, such as morning sickness. She felt very well and excited over the prospect of delivering their first child. When their son was born, the mood changed immediately and ominously when the doctors discovered the child was in serious physical distress. The next eighteen hours in the neonatal intensive care unit were filled with terrible dread and waiting.

In the end, their long-awaited and cherished firstborn son died, despite the best efforts of modern medicine. They were shocked and devastated. Words could not express how this traumatic reversal of fortunes had changed their lives forever in a single day.

The second example comes from the case of my wife, Marla, and me. A routine sonogram at 15 weeks turned out not so routine. The doctor gave this warning: "There's a problem with the baby." Further testing revealed that our son had a genetic abnormality that resulted in multiple problems, including an inoperable, fatal heart defect.

In short, knowledgeable doctors using the very best high-tech equipment told us that our son could not survive outside the uterus. His medical problems were considered "incompatible with life," and the doctor twice mentioned terminating the pregnancy. For faith-based and personal reasons, we chose to carry the pregnancy to full term. Thus, we faced the birth of a child we knew would die. All we could do was wait, watch, and love this boy as best we could in whatever time we had. We named him Anthony Francis while he was still in the womb.

If your child is stillborn or dies shortly after birth for reasons that could not be foreseen, you face the problem of unexpectedness. When your baby's death is unexpected, many questions haunt you. How could this have happened? What if you had done things differently? Where is God? What do you tell people? How do you inform the baby's grandparents and siblings? What are you supposed to do with the nursery? Will you still take leave from work? Do you return the baby's gifts or do you keep them for another child? Why was this child who meant so much taken so soon? What about all your long-term hopes and dreams for this child? Take time to sort out these questions and deal only with those requiring an immediate answer or decision, such as informing relatives and making arrangements with your employer.

Parents whose deceased newborns were treated in a neonatal intensive care unit may feel even worse that their child's short life was tangled in a maze of medical equipment and procedures. The possibility that their baby suffered leads to feelings of helplessness and guilt.

Anthony's case was different. The doctors identified his extensive medical problems early in the pregnancy. We understood that he could not live long after birth because his physical defects were so severe. His death was unwanted, but it was not unexpected.

In situations such as this, parents often experience anticipatory grief. This means parents start the grief process before their newborn child actually dies because they "see it coming." When feelings of anticipatory grief occur, they are considered natural and normal. Parents are trying to accommodate themselves to the inevitability of their child's death. While anticipatory grieving does not eliminate the hurting, for some parents, the pain is easier to bear.

How Can I Cope When I've Lost Someone I Loved So Much?

The special kinship between a parent and child is one of the strongest bonds in nature. Infants are helpless and totally dependent; they cannot survive on their own. Parents feed, care, protect, and nurture their offspring to ensure that the human family will be preserved. The intense feelings you have for your child are designed to guarantee that you provide this vital care. These same intense feelings are the source of your pain and anguish now that your child has died. In other words, the strength of your love determines the depth of your grief when your child is lost.

Whether your child was stillborn or died as a newborn does not change the fact that you are a parent. Death, whether unexpected or anticipated, does not invalidate your relationship with your child. You need to do the things a parent does for a new child:

- Hold her.
- Give her a name.
- Confirm she is yours and claim her as your own.
- Examine her little body and take inventory of which features resemble you or your family.
- Dress her.
- Take photographs, preserve a lock of hair, or make handprints and footprints.
- Marvel at the unique creation she is.
- Talk to her, sing to her, coo over her.
- Love her.

Remember, she is still your child and you have every right to be with her. Take your time being with her. Cherish your time together. It's the only time you will ever have to care for her physically. In most health care facilities, the professional staff will be sensitive to your needs and desires as a bereaved parent. If you feel unduly rushed, simply let the staff know that you are taking the time with your baby that you will never have again.

One of the most important things you can do is have your child baptized, if time allows. You will be comforted that your child received this sacrament. If your child died before he could be baptized, pray to God in this moment, committing the child to God's eternal love.

When deciding who should inform relatives and friends of your loss, follow your intuition. Telling others directly opens the opportunity for you to begin receiving support and condolences. On the other hand, if you feel burdened, ask a close friend or relative to inform others. You may also ask one of your health care providers, such as a nurse, or your pastor to help. This way, you can focus your concern on your deceased child and what you need to do for him.

How Do I Make Final Arrangements?

Sadly, you are required to make final arrangements for your child—something no parent wants to do. Should you choose burial, this means selecting a child-size coffin. Some hospitals will provide at no cost a modest coffin specifically for infants or newborns, or your funeral director can assist you in securing one. Some parents prefer to purchase a coffin through Internet sources or from direct suppliers. While such tasks may seem morbid, think of it as a labor of love that, as a parent, you have the privilege to do for your child.

Most cemeteries have special sections set aside with small plots for infant burials. Also, many cemeteries permit burial of small children adjacent to an adult family member. Cremated remains are often buried in the same plot with an adult family member. Again, a pastor or funeral director would be able to help you with these decisions. Don't be afraid to ask about these arrangements.

If you are planning a funeral or memorial service, you must consider who will participate, where it will be held and what the service will include. Ask your pastor for suggestions and guidelines regarding the death of an infant. In addition to hearing the comfort of God's Word through the Scriptures, including music in your service may be soothing.

Being involved in final arrangements is actually helpful. Clinical studies indicate that those who actively participate in planning their loved ones' funeral and burial services feel more comforted in their grief and adapt better later. Furthermore, making these arrangements is a tangible way of loving and caring for the physical needs of your lost child.

Some mothers are sick or hospitalized following the delivery of their deceased child and may not have had an opportunity to participate in planning services. These mothers often feel left out of a very important parenting task and may have resentment. While the events cannot be reversed, mothers should feel free to talk about their feelings with trusted friends or counselors, rather than suppress their emotions.

Why Do I Feel Jealous and Empty When I See Other Mothers and Babies?

Among the worst feelings bereaved parents experience is a terrible sense of emptiness. Sometimes this feeling has been described as "empty arms." This refers to wanting to hold and love a child who is not there. If you are a mother who has a child stillborn or has a newborn die, these feelings can be especially strong. Your body recognizes that you have delivered a baby and responds accordingly. As your milk comes in, for example, you ache to nurse the child you bore. But the baby is not there. Your own physical recovery from childbirth may be slower, and your pain level more intense. Such symptoms remind you further of your loss, and, with no new child to focus on, you do not have natural distractions from your pain.

Some parents find themselves intensely jealous of other couples with surviving children. Such feelings may not seem socially acceptable. They may be difficult to acknowledge—even to yourself. Nonetheless, if you feel jealous or resentful, confide in your partner or a sympathetic relative or friend. Discussing your emotions with someone you trust lessens these feelings and you will usually feel better after getting it off your chest.

Points to Remember

1. Unexpected stillbirth is devastating and feels terribly unfair. Expect to feel raw emotions of anger, betrayal, denial, and sadness.

2. Take time to sort out the many questions haunting you. Deal only with issues that require immediate attention.

3. Parents who know beforehand that their baby will have fatal health problems may begin the grieving process before the baby's birth. This is called "anticipatory grief." Although it doesn't eliminate the hurt, the pain is easier to bear.

4. The depth of your grief shows the strength of your love for your lost child.

5. Even though your child died, you are still a parent. Ignore comments from people who tell you otherwise.

6. Perform the tasks you would have done for your child had she lived: hold her, dress her, name her, talk to her. Take your time with her because this will be your only time together.

7. If it was not possible to baptize your child while she was still alive, pray to commend her to God's loving care.

8. Be involved in planning the funeral service or memorial.

9. Feelings of jealousy, resentment, and "empty arms" are part of the grief process. Talk about your feelings with a trusted friend or relative.

CHAPTER 3

For the Mother

A mother's attachment to her baby is something special from the beginning. From the first moment you realized, or suspected, that you were pregnant, you began to plan and prepare for your baby. Getting ready meant quietly mobilizing every part of yourself: physical, emotional, mental, and spiritual.

Losing your baby through miscarriage, stillbirth, or newborn death sends major shocks through your system. Your total being is in anguish. You feel grief in your body, in your heart, in your mind, and in your soul. The pain may flow throughout and tears may express a flood of sorrows. You do not want to give up your baby. You are in mourning—utterly and completely.

Why Do I Feel as if a Part of Me Has Died?

As a mother, your life is never completely your own. You choose to share it in an intimate, life-giving way with your children. Because your child is such an important part of who you are, your feelings of loss are likely to be much greater when your baby dies than when you suffer other losses. Other mothers understand this intuitively, and their support of you during this tragic time can be especially comforting.

Allow yourself to grieve. For bereaved mothers, grieving is very physical. Crying is considered a healthy expression of grief. Some fear that once the tears start flowing, they will never stop. Yet the truth is that tears usually come in waves, run their course, and subside naturally.

How Do I Calm Myself When I Need to Be Strong?

There will be times when you need to quiet yourself in order to handle things, attend to your partner, deal with other children, or just take some much-needed rest. To create a sense of calm, consider these recommendations:

• Regulate your breathing. Take deep breaths, hold them, and then blow out the air slowly and deliberately.

• Read the Bible, particularly selected Psalms or the Gospel of John.

• Repeat the Lord's Prayer or favorite hymns.

• Take a brisk walk (with your doctor's permission). This increases your blood flow, helps your breathing, and clears your mind.

Am I Still a Mother, Even Though My Baby Died?

Absolutely, positively yes! Even if you had a miscarriage a short time into your pregnancy, you are still a mother. You conceived this child and carried her inside your body for her entire natural life. Most important you loved her with a love that only a parent can fully know. That's what a mother does for her child.

If your baby was stillborn or died as a newborn, his death does not erase the fact that you are his mother. Motherhood is a wonderful privilege because it allows you to participate fully in the earthly creation of another person. Yes, there is a great deal more that you would have liked to have done for your child. It is deeply regrettable that you will not have that chance. But, what may be missing from the future does not cancel what you have done today. You have conceived, carried, and given birth to a child.

Yes, you are still a mother—forever.

Why Doesn't My Baby's Father Understand My Pain?

During this difficult time, remember that you are still a partner. Just as you still need your baby's father, he still needs you. Please recognize that a father often experiences loss of a baby in a manner different from the mother. He may need some help to understand your feelings. Sharing your thoughts and feelings honestly, and relying on your mutual faith—perhaps even reading this book together—are ways that you can stay close as a couple through this crisis.

Points to Remember

1. No matter the circumstances, losing a baby is a shock to your entire body. Grief will flood all parts of your being—emotionally, physically, mentally, and spiritually.

2. Support from other mothers during this tragic time can be especially comforting.

3. Give yourself permission to grieve. Be assured, however, that tears will flow in torrents, run their course, and subside.

4. Calm yourself by breathing deeply, repeating a familiar prayer or verse, or taking a brisk walk.

5. Never forget that you are still a mother even though your baby died. What may be missing from the future does not cancel what you have done today.

6. Share your feelings honestly with your baby's father. He is grieving, too, although he may not show it outwardly.

CHAPTER 4

For the Father

Fathers sometimes feel forgotten when miscarriage or stillbirth happens.

In chapter 2, I told the story of my son, Anthony. Just 15 weeks into the pregnancy, doctors warned us that our son had a life-threatening genetic abnormality. My wife and I were devastated. We knew he could not live outside of the uterus; yet, we decided to carry him to full term. He died shortly after birth.

In the days immediately after his death, family and friends frequently asked me: "How's Marla doing?" I knew they were concerned about Marla's feelings and were probably trying to gauge what to say to her. But this reminded me that I was expected to protect her and act as the head of the household, even when our household was in mourning. That is what fathers are supposed to do.

Why Don't I Feel the Overwhelming Sadness That My Baby's Mother Feels?

Fathers bond with children in different ways from mothers. For many fathers, an unborn baby is an abstract being. The link between father and child tends to be more intellectual. A father knows the child is there, but does not feel the presence of the child as much as the mother, who feels the baby's movements and weight inside her body. Once the baby is born and the interaction begins, fathers bond more tightly.

Some fathers feel awkward or even guilty about the fact that their initial grief seems muted compared to what the mother feels. If you find yourself feeling less sadness and less emotion than your baby's mother, you are not doing anything wrong. It probably means that, as the father, you did not have the chance to grow as close to your baby as your partner did.

Not every father feels this muted grief. It depends on how much the father bonded with the baby. Fathers who have not completely bonded find it difficult to grieve the loss of a baby they did not really know. Masculine grief is not always expressed outwardly. Because our culture emphasizes men maintaining their composure, not every bereaved father is comfortable showing sadness or crying at funerals, even his own baby's.

What Is the Best Way for a Father to Grieve?

Masculine grief is often expressed by doing. Doing something constructive, such as making final arrangements, taking over some household chores, or even washing the cars before the funeral, helps a father channel emotions into concrete activities. Doing something constructive helps counteract the terrible feelings of helplessness.

With my own loss of Anthony, among the most important things I did in my grief was to carry my son—literally. I was the only pallbearer required at the church and at the cemetery. I considered it a father's honor and duty; I would not have had it any other way.

Remember, being present physically and emotionally is also important. It takes much strength to make yourself available to others who need your presence and support after your child has died.

Am I Still a Father, Even if I Don't Feel Like I Bonded With the Baby?

Even though your child is gone, you are still a father. Fatherhood is not so much about a biological act as it is about raising, supporting, and loving a child. You were prepared fully to do just that. However, tragic circumstances occurred, and you never really got the complete chance. Losing your child does not cancel your identity as a father. You remain a father to this child because you stood ready and willing to do all a father does—and more.

How Do I Help My Baby's Mother?

Even though your child has died, you are still a partner. Your baby's mother desperately needs you. She needs to know that she is not alone. She needs to know that you still love her. She needs to feel your love when her grief is breaking her in two. Please do not isolate yourself, but be present. Be the partner she needs. No one shares your pain and disappointment as profoundly as she does. For this reason, going through the loss of a child together can strengthen your relationship and can serve as a beautiful testament to the memory of your deceased child.

Points to Remember

1. Fathers bond with their babies differently from mothers. A father's grief may appear muted, but fathers still grieve.

2. If you feel less sadness than the child's mother, you have not done anything wrong. It means you did not have an opportunity to bond closely with the lost baby.

3. You are still a father even if your baby died. You were willing and able to do all the things a father does for his children.

4. Your baby's mother needs you during this difficult time. Reassure her that you still love her. She needs to feel your emotional and physical presence.

Chapter 5

For the Families

(Grandparents and Siblings)

The death of a baby affects all family members. Because each member is connected in the family network, grief touches each one. Grandparents and siblings of the lost child may be particularly affected. Promoting family unity through communication and mutual understanding is important at the time of death.

For Grandparents

How Can I Help My Adult Child Bear This Heavy Burden?

In previous generations, women privately endured pain and loss after miscarriage. Because many families were larger, the loss of a baby was considered "insignificant." Mothers were often told: "You have other children to love," or that miscarriage was "just part of nature." They were told "not to dwell on the past," and to focus on their living children.

When a baby was stillborn, some families and medical professionals discouraged a mother from seeing or holding her dead child, believing that she would be too upset. If the baby was given a funeral, the child was soon "forgotten" and no one ever mentioned the loss again. The truth is—even generations ago—mothers did feel loss and grief, but such issues were rarely discussed openly in "polite" company.

Grandparents who lived through those times may recall such reactions and ideas. Thankfully, bereaved parents today are encouraged to tell their stories, express their grief, and describe what their deceased child meant to them. When your adult children suffer the loss of their own children through miscarriage, stillbirth, or newborn death, they may turn to you for comfort and want to talk about their loss. Sharing their pain in an understanding, sympathetic way is a very natural way of supporting an adult child, and it's something you should do willingly.

Is "Grandparent Grief" Real, or Is It Merely a Myth?

This "would-have-been" grandchild carried a great deal of meaning and legacy for you as a grandparent. The same kinship bond in nature that ties parents to their children also ties you to your grandchildren. Grandparent grief is not always recognized when your son or daughter loses a child, but it is real nevertheless. The loss of a grandchild leaves you with your own pain in addition to the sorrow your son or daughter carries. You hurt for your child and for yourself. That's why grandparent grief is sometimes thought of as "double grief."

The grief is compounded if grandparents themselves suffered miscarriage or stillbirth years ago. Because these losses were not readily acknowledged, your adult child's loss may stir up your own dormant grief feelings. For example, one grandmother recalled strong feelings of grief, shame, and resentment about her experiences decades before when she lost a baby. She talked about how medical personnel and her family tried to protect her by downplaying the events. This grandmother had to vent her past feelings to a nurse before she could help her own grieving adult child.

Why Do I Feel Downhearted, as if Hope Is Gone?

As a grandparent, you will grieve for many reasons. Your expectations and hopes for the future are linked to your grandchildren. Grandchildren are a continuation of the precious cycle of life, and you are comforted by the realization that your family will live on after you are gone. When a grandchild dies, this is jeopardized.

Grandchildren are a major source of joy, which now is gone. You do not have grandchild pictures to show your friends. You are not "needed" in that special way a grandparent is. You are not able to bask in your grandchild's unconditional love. You cannot delight in your grandchild while remaining relatively free of responsibility for her. When you lose a grandchild, a part of your legacy seems lost.

Today's families are smaller than in generations past. Many couples have only two or three children; some, only one. Childbearing is often postponed while couples complete their education or establish careers. When a couple is ready to start a family, a miscarriage or problem pregnancy disrupts a carefully crafted life script. Parents of a childbearing adult have difficulty witnessing their child delay pregnancy longer than seems prudent or fail to consider that everything in life does not turn out picture perfect. Remember, you cannot control your child's decisions; you can only be there to help should something go wrong.

As a Father, Why Do I Feel So Helpless When My Adult Daughter Is in Pain?

Fathers of adult daughters often take on the task of "fixing things." When your daughter was young, you kissed scraped knees, repaired broken bikes, and hugged away bruised feelings. When she became a young woman, you probably helped with car repairs, financial shortages, and advice on relationships or business matters. That's what dads are for.

However, when your daughter has a miscarriage or stillbirth, you can't "fix it." You feel helpless and confused. To complicate the issue, you may know few details about the pregnancy itself and you may have very little information to help you understand what happened. Please remember that where your grieving child is concerned, "being there" is often the biggest help you can provide. Your presence and attention matter most. As the concerned father and grandfather, you can exercise spiritual leadership by offering to lead the family in prayer for God's guidance, mercy, comfort and loving presence.

"Into every life some pain shall come." By virtue of longevity and life experience, grandparents know the truth of this saying. You have learned that life has its share of sadness as well as happiness and that most disappointments loom largest at their onset. Knowing this can help you with your own grief and help you comfort and reassure your child after a miscarriage, stillbirth, or newborn death.

For Siblings

How Do I Tell My Other Children That We Won't Have a Baby to Bring Home?

Having another baby is an exciting time for children. Together, you and your children planned for this new baby: choosing a name, setting up the baby's room, deciding who would help with chores after the baby was born. The siblings may have attended a class to help them welcome this new brother or sister. Or maybe you had just announced that a new family member would be added in a few months. Sadly, the joy surrounding these preparations has been cut short. In the midst of your grief, you realize that you must help your children learn that a new baby will not be coming home.

No matter their ages, your children will feel your sadness. They are also concerned about whether Mom and Dad will be all right. Expressing your grief through crying and holding or hugging them will comfort you both and give them much-needed reassurance.

Death is a complex concept for children to grasp. They handle it differently, depending on their age. Younger children ask countless questions to help them place everything in concrete terms. Provide them simple examples from nature, such as how plants and animals grow and then die. You can also use as a foundation their knowledge about God and His love. If you need help with what to tell your young children, turn to your pastor for guidance. Your older children may be more concerned about Mom and Dad's health and happiness.

If the cause of death is known, explain this to your children in terms that they can understand. If the cause is unknown, honestly tell them you don't know why the baby died. Telling a young child that the baby was "lost" can be very confusing; your child may think that the baby will be "found" or "come back" home. Truthful explanations build trust and help alleviate potential feelings of guilt.

How Can I Help My Children Cope With the Baby's Death?

Many siblings worry that they may have caused the loss. Some may blame themselves because of their actions or because they had mixed feelings about having a sibling. Children should be reassured that they are not to blame.

Your child's behavior may change: regressing to more baby-like behavior, withdrawing, or even becoming aggressive. They may be reacting to unspoken grief or fear about losing a parent. Children may be overwhelmed and apprehensive about the sudden presence of distant relatives and strangers. Loving support from you, grandparents, and familiar family members can help children express openly their grief and fears.

Finding a way for siblings to participate in the memorial service helps them express their grief. For younger children, have them select a toy or religious article—or draw a picture—to place in the baby's coffin.

Older children may help pick the baby's burial outfit, choose a song or Scripture passage, or write a poem. Offer suggestions to them and follow their cues. Remember, they are grieving, too, in their own special ways.

The following story illustrates how the death of a baby affects siblings for many years.

Ann's Story

As a nurse and a mother, I sometimes find that sharing my story about loss in our family gives some insight to how siblings respond. When I was 10 years old, my mother was pregnant with her eighth child. It was my turn to be the "helper" in caring for a brand new baby sister or brother. My mom had never experienced a pregnancy loss. We had no idea what was to happen.

Mom was two weeks from her due date when she went into labor. Each time the phone rang, we all eavesdropped with anticipation as my grandmother answered the phone. However, this time Grandma turned away from us and, in a low tone, consoled the caller on the other end—my dad. Grandma placed the phone back on the receiver. The announcement was not like other times when Mom had a new baby. Mom had delivered our sister, Marguerite Elizabeth, and the baby did not survive the birth.

Sadness surrounded us, and we wondered how we should act when my mom came home from the hospital. I wanted nothing to hurt her or my dad. It seemed best not to talk about the baby because this made them cry.

A week later, I confessed to my older sister that I thought I was the cause of Marguerite's death because I had upset Mom a few days before Marguerite was born. We were both crying. Then she confessed to me that she thought she was the cause of Marguerite's death for the same reason. What a cleansing relief we both experienced at that moment because we both realized that this was out of our hands and in God's.

Not a year goes by that I don't think of Marguerite on her birthday.

Points to Remember

For Grandparents

1. Attitudes about miscarriage and stillbirth have changed over the decades. Your adult child may grieve in a manner different from people of your generation.

2. Listen supportively as your adult child describes the loss.

3. Grandparents and grandchildren share a special bond. You as a grandparent will also suffer a unique kind of loss. "Grandparent grief" is real.

4. You may feel that your hopes and expectations for the future are gone with the lost grandchild.

5. As a grandparent, you have the advantage of experience and the wisdom of age. You know firsthand that life has its share of great joys and deep sorrows. This will help you comfort and reassure your adult children.

For Siblings

1. Siblings—no matter their age—feel their parents' grief and sadness.

2. Depending on their ages, children will understand death differently. Simple, honest answers, appropriate for the child's age, are the best response.

3. Children may believe that they caused the baby's death. Reassure them that they did not.

4. Find age-appropriate ways to let siblings participate in memorial or funeral services.

Chapter 6

Going on From Here

Why? Why our baby? Why us? Why now? These are the hardest questions to answer about the death of a child.

I know that I struggled with these questions concerning our son, Anthony. Even though he was born alive, Anthony lived only a few minutes because of his heart problems. His fragile body could not sustain life outside the womb. In the short time Anthony was alive, we baptized him, held him, took pictures, and—most important—loved him. We did not release his body for another three hours until we had had a chance to finish bonding and to grieve.

How Can I Accept Something I Don't Understand?

When it came to the "why" questions concerning Anthony's brief life and death, a Scripture passage proved particularly helpful.

Recommended by a friend, this Scripture gave me much to think about: "However, as it is written: 'No eye has seen, no ear has heard, no mind has conceived what God has prepared for those who love him'" (1 Cor. 2:9). My friend helped me grasp the fact that some things go unanswered in this life—like many of the "why" questions. As much as we may strive for answers, there will never be satisfactory explanations for why things happen in this life as they do. Instead, we wait for the answers in the next life, while maintaining our faith and hope in God.

In my work as a clinical psychologist, I have seen some grieving parents struggle relentlessly to answer every "why" question about their baby's death. They are riveted to the idea that if they can understand it, then they can accept it. For some, the pursuit of answers becomes an unhealthy obsession. Acceptance of your baby's death often comes in the absence of all the answers.

One of the most profound statements about accepting death I have ever heard came from a 9-year-old boy with terminal cancer. Trying to reassure his own mother before he died, he said to her: "Once you accept it, then you can understand it. Once you understand it, then you can go on with your life."

The lesson is clear. Acceptance leads to understanding and going on from here means accepting your child's death—even without all the answers.

I have also come to understand that the value and significance of my son's life could not be measured adequately by his length of time in this world. During his brief life, Anthony deeply touched everyone who became aware of our family's situation. The power of love transcended time. Anthony's impact was linked to how much he was loved and to the love he brought into the world, just by being himself.

So, Where Do I Go From Here?

Recent bereavement studies have revealed a fascinating finding—those who recognize some good resulting from the death of their loved one seem to cope better with their grief. On the surface, this sounds like common sense. Yet keep in mind that for the "good result" to be comforting, it has to be meaningful to the bereaved person. When others try to point out the proverbial "silver lining" in the cloud, they often miss the mark. Platitudes such as "You have an angel in heaven," or, "She's in a better place," rarely comfort a parent who is grieving the loss of a cherished child. These remarks are shallow and inconsequential to parents who feel their child has been ripped away forever.

What does comfort bereaved parents? Here are some ways how bereaved parents see that the world has become a better place because of their baby:

- Knowing that this child's life (and death) had a positive effect on someone else.
- Connecting more deeply with one's faith.
- Having families or communities draw closer dur-

ing this crisis.

• Discovering their own wisdom or personal strength, especially if that parent uses the experience to help someone else or to make positive life changes.

In my own situation, actively seeking some good out of the tragedy of Anthony's impending death led Marla and me to initiate a memorial project. In lieu of flowers, we requested that memorials be made toward establishing a children's library at our church. The response was very generous. Knowing that many young children will benefit from the donations made in Anthony's memory has given us a clear sense of good emerging from the sadness.

Should We Try to Have Another Child?

Anxiety and self-doubt may linger after miscarriage, stillbirth, or newborn death. Many parents are fearful about becoming pregnant again. The pain of loss is too intense, and they are afraid of another unhappy ending. A mother might question her ability to carry a child to term and deliver a healthy baby. The fears are expected and understandable, but how you deal with them makes all the difference. You do not need to decide right away whether you want to have another child. Do not feel pressured. Give yourself and your partner a chance to grieve. Then, with your doctor, evaluate what happened. You, your partner, and your doctor can discuss what medical risks, if any, are involved in getting pregnant again.

Give yourself time to make this decision. Listen to your doctor. Listen to your partner. Listen to your heart. Listen to God. Then decide.

Points to Remember

1. No one can really answer why tragic events occur. Sometimes they just happen and we never know why in our lifetimes.

2. The length of a child's life on earth is no indication of her worth. Your baby's impact is linked to how much you loved her and to the love she brought into the world just through being herself.

3. Acceptance leads to understanding, and going on from here means accepting your child's death—even without all the answers.

4. Those who recognize some good resulting from the death of their loved one seem to cope better with their grief. Grieving parents find comfort in knowing that their child's life—no matter how brief—had positive effects on someone else.

5. Disregard platitudes such as "You have an angel in heaven," or, "He's in a better place."

6. Self-doubts and anxiety about future pregnancies are understandable and expected. Take your time making a decision about having another child.

Conclusion

Our fondest wish is that it would never be necessary for anyone to read this book. Sadly, babies sometimes die, and medical science has not been able to prevent it.

We hope this book has brought you some comfort. Parts of it may have been difficult to read. If so, come back to it later. Different sections may become more meaningful; or you may gain insight that escaped you earlier. Such is the nature of the continual process of grieving.

In closing, here is a final thought. Those who grieve are those who love. Without loving your lost child and wanting to be close to him, there would be no loss when he died. Your grief itself is a tribute to your love for your baby. You can further honor your deceased child by remembering fondly what she has meant to you and by living life fully aware that people matter more than things, and that every moment of our existence is a precious gift to be used wisely and well.

God bless you.

My Reflections